TODD FULTZ

JOURNAL

Your
YEAR OF LITTLE VICTORIES

VICTORY
PRESS

Your Year of Little Victories / by Todd Fultz

ISBN: 978-0-9831311-2-0

Cover & Interior: Lookout Design, Inc.

Author Photo: Ricky Lesser

Printed by Bayport Printing House, Inc., Bayport, Minnesota

Victory Press, LLC

4730 Neal Avenue North

Stillwater, MN 55082

10 11 12 13 14 15   (BPH)   10 9 8 7 6 5 4 3 2 1

Dedication

--- ⚙ ---

This book is dedicated to

MARY, TIMMY, & MADELINE.

You can accomplish anything.

Introduction

--- ❖ ---

THE TROPHY CASE

In all my years of football, I've never seen a team that has a trophy case full of their biggest defeats.

No, they put out the trophies, the titles, the photos of epic wins and great players. They put out the awards, the best and brightest.

Every team has wins and every team has losses in their history: that's the nature of the game. But putting up a trophy case full of losses would send the wrong signal. It would say this is a bad team. We can't win.

Trophy cases focus on what's positive. They turn a blind eye to the bad and the ugly, focusing solely on the good. The pain of injuries, the grueling two-a-day practices have been swept into the dustbin of history: what's remembered now are the glorious results.

This workbook format in itself is nothing new. What makes this book unique is that we are only going to look at the positives. Think of this book as your trophy case. It should do for you what a trophy case does for the team: commemorate wins, great moments that you want to preserve. In bad times you can remember the good things you've done, and think of the good things you'll do in the future.

We're going to focus on your little victories. Looking back on our lives we tend to think of big victories (getting married, buying your first house, that promotion you've been working toward for five years), but it's the little victories that get us to the big ones.

A little victory is just one of the many small victories along the way to achieving a larger goal. It is the momentum of those little victories that carry you on the journey to get to that goal. Little victories got me through a 120 mile per hour head on collision and back on my feet, and they can help you too.

Todd

"At St. John's, when we watched game films John would focus on the great plays or, as he called them, 'the classics.'" We didn't watch mistakes."

Power of a Positive Outlook

━━━━━━━━━━━━━ ✿ ━━━━━━━━━━━━━

THE CLASSICS

That approach creates a confidence and positive attitude that you *will* succeed because you have seen yourself do it. John Gagliardi is the greatest college football coach in the history of college football but, more importantly, he has given the thousands of kids who have played for him even better coaching in life. Because this focus on the classics has helped me so much, I hope you will use it as well. Focus on your classics each day and don't worry about the small stuff.

Remember my trophy case analogy from the introduction? Your thoughts and memories about yourself are like that trophy case. Remember the best of the best.

1. How does this relate to your life?

. . . .

. . . .

. . . .

. . . .

. . . .

. . . .

. . . .

2. What were your little victories this week?

. . . .

. . . .

. . . .

. . . .

. . . .

. . . .

. . . .

"We were never promised life would be fair.
We were not guaranteed everything would work out.
We were simply given the opportunity to participate in life,
and life is full of incredible possibilities."

Finding Meaning in Suffering

———————————— ✺ ————————————

LIFE IS NOT FAIR

We can choose our direction in life, and we can choose the people we spend time with. Surround yourself with the people who find the opportunity in life. They will help you to go places, and in turn you will help them.

I wish we had an unlimited amount of time to get this crazy life figured out. But, since we do not, now would be a great time to take advantage of it. Regardless of what has happened in your life, each day is new and full of possibilities and opportunity. Most of all, it is a wonderful gift.

1. How does this relate to your life?

2. What were your little victories this week?

> *"Certainly, athletes must have a dream that they break down first into long-term objectives and then further into short term goals."*
> *– Damon Burton*

One Step at a Time

FIRST DOWNS

In football, the goal of the offense is to march the ball down the field and score a touchdown. The operative word here is *march*.

Now and again, the quarterback will make a long touchdown pass or a running back will break free, but the vast majority of touchdowns come after a number of incremental goals are met. Those incremental goals are first downs. The offense can then say, "Just ten more yards." After they get those yards, they once again say, "Just ten more yards."

If they continue to execute and meet their goals, before you know it they are in the end zone. If, on the other hand, they started on their own twenty yard line and saw that they had eighty yards to go against a tough defense, the job would seem almost impossible.

1. How does this relate to your life?

. . . .

. . . .

. . . .

. . . .

. . . .

. . . .

. . . .

2. What were your little victories this week?

. . . .

. . . .

. . . .

. . . .

. . . .

. . . .

. . . .

. . . .

"It [a birthday invitation] makes me think about what I have that is dearest to me: am I doing a good job of sharing it with those around me?"

Gratitude

--- ❁ ---

SHARE THE WEALTH

I asked myself this question after my sweet little Madeline invited me to her birthday: ten times. At first I didn't understand why she asked me over and over, and then it dawned on me. As a three-year-old there was precious little she could control: but who she invited to her birthday party, that was her decision, and she was making it abundantly clear that she wanted me there.

That invitation meant so much to me: she was choosing me, choosing to share something very important to her with me. What an honor.

1. How does this relate to your life?

....

....

....

....

....

....

....

2. What were your little victories this week?

....

....

....

....

....

....

....

"Things are good here. I continue to be amazed at the wonderful support you have all provided. Each day I receive many e-mails, phone calls, and letters from friends, family, and people I have never met before."

Family and Friends

WHO WILL BE THERE FOR YOU?

There's a saying that has presumably been around for a long time, something we tell our kids when they're struggling to understand the nuances of relationships: to have a friend, be a friend.

I have been blessed with an outgoing personality. Growing up, I was grateful to be on some outstanding teams that gave me an opportunity to make friends for life. My parents modeled how to genuinely care for others, and I seem to have picked that up by osmosis. I try to live a full life with those around me and live without regrets.

I was incredibly thankful when the time came that I needed help. People came out of the woodwork to contribute in big ways and in little ways. They knew I would do (or maybe had done) the same for them. It was a beautiful thing.

Social support structures are crucial. There will come a time in our lives when we will need other people, and a time when those same people will need us. How are your social supports?

1. How does this relate to your life?

....

....

....

....

....

....

....

2. What were your little victories this week?

....

....

....

....

....

....

....

....

"There is always enough time in a day to do God's will."
– Roy Lessin

Gold Medals

———————— ⚙ ————————

DO WE SPEND OUR TIME WELL?

Ask most people their thoughts about time and you'll get one answer loud and clear: there's not enough of it. If only we had a twenty-six hour day, they'll say.

I remember a story from when I was in high school. I was talking to Bud Grant, the father of my football coach. I asked him if he'd been fishing. He replied that he had, and told me some great stories. Then he turned the question around: "Have you been fishing?"

I shook my head and said, "No Bud, I don't have time." He put his hands on my shoulders and looked me straight in the eye. "Todd, you make time."

What's most important to you? Think long and hard about that. That's where you should be spending your time.

1. How does this relate to your life?

. . . .

. . . .

. . . .

. . . .

. . . .

. . . .

. . . .

2. What were your little victories this week?

. . . .

. . . .

. . . .

. . . .

. . . .

. . . .

. . . .

"I get emotional each time I enter the Courage Center as I realize the potential of the day. The opportunity to take one step without using the bars is right there waiting. I hope to do it soon."

The Miracle of Life

———————— ✿ ————————

THE POTENTIAL IN EACH DAY

Each day when I walked into the Courage Center, I was working toward a goal: walking. I knew that each time I would get closer to my goal until one day I would achieve it. It was hard and painful work, but it was so worth it!

The Courage Center is filled with overachievers and that motivated me. Imagine what would have happened if I'd gone in with the intention of killing time. I'd still be struggling to reach my goals. Many times we don't try for things because we don't think they're possible. We aren't focused on the goals at hand or reaching for our potential: we're stuck in the same place. We kill time.

1. How does this relate to your life?

. . . .

. . . .

. . . .

. . . .

. . . .

. . . .

. . . .

2. What were your little victories this week?

. . . .

. . . .

. . . .

. . . .

. . . .

. . . .

. . . .

. . . .

"I thank God for continuing to fill you with such hope and faith for your future which allows you to share your deep words and thoughts of encouragement with the rest of us. That pretty well describes the word 'ministry' for me." – Phil Kadidlo

The Spiritual Life

HOPE WHEN FACING THE UNKNOWN

To me, trusting God means trusting that each experience has a purpose. God will bring hope from ashes and He will bring meaning from suffering. Our job is not to dwell on the negatives, but rather to be attentive to ways God might work in this situation.

God has not promised that we would face no evil—clearly we will. We are taught in the Lord's Prayer to ask that He "deliver us from evil." We have to pray for deliverance, cling to God, and look on the bright side.

1. How does this relate to your life?

....

....

....

....

....

....

....

2. What were your little victories this week?

....

....

....

....

....

....

....

....

"Along with that hernia came some pretty deep fears and depression. I saw how attitudes can be contagious. I saw how my mood was affecting my family. I knew I wanted to keep my spirits up, but this new visit to the hospital was a surprise and a severe struggle."

The Importance of Laughter

—————————— ⚙ ——————————

MOODS ARE CONTAGIOUS

Difficult situations will come our way: that is a guarantee. It's important to acknowledge these situations, but not to dwell on them. Laughter in times of adversity is a very healthy thing, lifting the spirits of all those who are going through it. I found time to say a funny line to my nurses: I found their laughter helped me as well.

While you may not find the humor in your situation, there's a vast supply of funny things out there. Watch a movie or hear a comic. Give yourself a break. It isn't always easy to seek out laughter, but it is worth the effort.

1. How does this relate to your life?

....

....

....

....

....

....

....

2. What were your little victories this week?

....

....

....

....

....

....

....

....

Soul Food

---❉---

PRAYING FOR OURSELVES

We often say we will pray for someone: hopefully we follow through on that promise. But how often are we conscious of praying for ourselves?

This is an essential part of growing closer to God. Theologians describe prayer as a dialogue with God. If that's so, it's an essential part of getting to know Him.

God wants us to talk to him about what's going on with us in the same way a loving father wants to hear from his children. We are to cast our cares upon Him, confess our sins to Him, to ask Him for strength. Sounds a lot like a good father, doesn't it?

1. How does this relate to your life?

. . . .

. . . .

. . . .

. . . .

. . . .

. . . .

. . . .

2. What were your little victories this week?

. . . .

. . . .

. . . .

. . . .

. . . .

. . . .

. . . .

*"Your stories, emails, words of encouragement, and the memories
of the days of youth keep me going . . . Please remember Dr. Ly today
in your prayers. And also please remember the man who hit me,
in your prayers as he recovers as well."*

Life Without Regrets

---·❖·---

NECESSITY OF FORGIVENESS

The other driver hit me head on at sixty miles per hour pulling out to pass a dump truck on a two lane road. That collision changed my life forever.

I could be angry at him, but why? What would it accomplish? Unforgiveness holds hostage the person who harbors it. And that's all it does. It eats at you from the inside.

If you're going to really enjoy life and get the most out of it that you can, forgiveness is an essential part of that puzzle. It doesn't mean that justice can't or won't be served, it just means that you let go of that person and that event. By setting them free, you set yourself free.

1. How does this relate to your life?

2. What were your little victories this week?

> *"It is the surmounting of obstacles that makes heroes."*
> *– Louis Kossuth*

Endurance

--- ✿ ---

THE M.A.S.H. UNIT

When Erica wrote that quote on our CaringBridge site, she was writing about the night I spent in the hospital on Day 11. They'd moved me out of ICU and the wing I was in was crazy. On that particular night, I roomed with a drunk guy who'd been stabbed in a bar fight. Though I was heavily medicated, I was still with it enough to be worried.

The doctor came in that night and said that he was worried about infection around my surgical incisions.

I was in a tough spot, but and I had two options: to fight and move forward or to give up and resign myself to the idea that I was a cripple, and an infected one to boot. I was taught to never give up: by my parents, by my coaches, by my friends. I had every reason to move forward, and so I did.

1. How does this relate to your life?

....

....

....

....

....

....

....

2. What were your little victories this week?

....

....

....

....

....

....

....

....

"It is not the mountain we conquer but ourselves."
– Sir Edmund Hillary

Finish Strong

---- ⚙ ----

THE AIR IS THINNER AT THE TOP

Sir Edmund Hillary was the first climber to reach the top of Mount Everest. *Time* magazine dubbed him one of the 100 most influential people of the 20th century.

After setting up base camp in March of 1953, Hillary climbed for *two months* before summiting on May 29. Imagine what those two months must have been like: unceasing wind and incredible cold. The nearer they got to the top, the harder the climb became and the worse conditions grew.

Hillary's quote is interesting. After making the greatest ascent in recorded history, he considers his primary triumph one of the will. He didn't conquer Everest: he conquered himself.

1. How does this relate to your life?

. . . .

. . . .

. . . .

. . . .

. . . .

. . . .

. . . .

2. What were your little victories this week?

. . . .

. . . .

. . . .

. . . .

. . . .

. . . .

. . . .

"I woke up today with the hope that I would find the energy and the right moment to try. I understood that it might not happen and I was OK with that."

Power of a Positive Outlook

HOPE AND ACCEPTANCE

September 28th was a special day for me. I had a lofty goal— to walk without my walker less than four months after the accident took place.

I was certainly going to give it my all, but I had to acknowledge that there were more factors in play than just the strength of my will. Would my muscles hold me up? Would there be problems with my surgically-reconstructed joints and bones?

As it turned out, I walked. It was amazing and beautiful. But if I hadn't walked, I would have figured out why and set a new goal to correct those issues and to walk. Advances don't always happen on the timeline we would prefer, but if we stay with it, they will come.

1. How does this relate to your life?

....

....

....

....

....

....

2. What were your little victories this week?

....

....

....

....

....

....

....

....

"The pain is a pain, but hey, every day is beautiful.
I sleep next to my wife each night and our three beautiful children
run and jump on our bed each morning. Life is pretty darn good."

Finding Meaning in Suffering

❋

DESPITE THE PAIN,
EVERY DAY IS BEAUTIFUL

I live now with chronic pain in my ankle, back and hips. It will probably never go away.

So what? That's one side of things. The other is that I love what I do, I love my family and my friends, my home, my life. I feel incredibly blessed. I don't let chronic body pain take me away from all that is good and all that is possible. I choose to fight through it and participate in life.

1. How does this relate to your life?

. . . .

. . . .

. . . .

. . . .

. . . .

. . . .

. . . .

2. What were your little victories this week?

. . . .

. . . .

. . . .

. . . .

. . . .

. . . .

. . . .

. . . .

*"I could do whatever I set my mind to:
I was proving this to myself daily."*

One Step at a Time

❋

YOU CAN DO THE THINGS
YOU PUT YOUR MIND TO

They had a foam balance beam at Courage Center. That thing was my nemesis, but I resolved to beat it. I would walk down it. And I did.

I attempted the bar multiple times before I made it. Each time I got a little closer. Each time I learned something about how to do it. And each time I got closer, I gained greater resolve and confidence that I could, in fact, do it.

It was hard at the beginning, but that initial block can't be the end of it. The power of a firm will and an intent mind is very great indeed.

1. How does this relate to your life?

. . . .

. . . .

. . . .

. . . .

. . . .

. . . .

. . . .

2. What were your little victories this week?

. . . .

. . . .

. . . .

. . . .

. . . .

. . . .

. . . .

. . . .

*"Children have a gift for bringing out those smiles,
even when situations appear bleak. I was so grateful to have
some little comedians running around my house."*

Gratitude

❄

APPRECIATE WHAT YOU HAVE

Life is busy now: often too busy. Sometimes we're going so fast we
don't see the people around us, the people who matter the most.

I certainly appreciated my family when I was laying there flat on my
back, not sure if I was going to live or die. Don't get me wrong, I've
always appreciated my family, always made choices that would be
good for our family, but that sort of experience sharpens the focus
even further.

There's great value in learning from another's experiences without
having to go through them yourself. I'm hoping you can learn this
invaluable lesson from my experiences.

1. How does this relate to your life?

....

....

....

....

....

....

....

2. What were your little victories this week?

....

....

....

....

....

....

....

....

*"This deer hunting trip is more about fellowship
than anything else. It's a created event that turned into a tradition,
and it became a tradition that brought people together."*

Family and Friends

--- ⚙ ---

TRADITION

As a kid, I remember going out to the garage after my dad would return from a deer hunting trip, and I would find an enormous buck. It impressed me and I knew I wanted to participate in this tradition myself one day. The idea of missing even one year of this tradition with my dad was unfathomable. I knew I was going to Wyoming with the guys.

This tradition is something I put great value on. It has brought me, my dad, and our friends close together in a way that playing cards or watching football never could. We make the effort to get away and spend time together, and it's a beautiful thing.

I believe traditions are necessary for families to bond and to have a firm foundation.

1. How does this relate to your life?

....

....

....

....

....

....

....

2. What were your little victories this week?

....

....

....

....

....

....

....

....

"Life shrinks or expands in proportion to one's courage."
- Anaïs Nin

Gold Medals

THE FIGHTING SPIRIT

Often when people wrote in on my CaringBridge site, they'd comment on my fighting spirit. There are a few reasons for this: I saw my brother, Tim, fight cancer twenty-five years ago, and that has always stayed with me. As an athlete, I learned that anything good—anything you were going to achieve—you were going to have to fight for. A wide receiver isn't much good if he goes down after the first hit.

Lastly, I had a lot to fight for! I had my family and friends. I literally fought to get my life back. If I hadn't put up a fight, I don't know where I'd be today. Frankly, I'd rather not think about it. When we love something, that's when we must fight the hardest to keep it.

1. How does this relate to your life?

. . . .

. . . .

. . . .

. . . .

. . . .

. . . .

. . . .

2. What were your little victories this week?

. . . .

. . . .

. . . .

. . . .

. . . .

. . . .

. . . .

"Making the time for these moments isn't always easy,
but words cannot express how important it is.
If we don't clear the space for scrambled eggs and bacon
in the morning, it won't be there."

The Miracle of Life

TREASURE YOUR TIME

Starting the day with a hearty breakfast and conversation in the kitchen is a tradition I have always been excited to pass on to my kids. When I was a kid, my mom always made me eggs or toast or oatmeal and talked to me about the day before I walked out into the world. I remember those mornings vividly and, during my recovery period, I didn't want my handicap to stop me from getting a good breakfast in my kids' bellies before they left for school.

It's a simple thing really. It's just breakfast. It takes ten minutes, but if you add those ten minutes up over a month, you have 300 minutes of quality time with your kids. You'll have thirty chances to speak truth into their lives that you wouldn't have had otherwise.

1. How does this relate to your life?

....

....

....

....

....

....

2. What were your little victories this week?

....

....

....

....

....

....

....

....

"But those who hope in the Lord will renew their strength.
They will soar on wings like eagles; they will run
and not grow weary, they will walk and not be faint."
- Isaiah 40:31

The Spiritual Life

--- ⚙ ---

SOURCE OF DAILY STRENGTH

I often had days during my recovery where the whole thing felt overwhelming. I just didn't have much left in the tank. I'm sure you've had that feeling too.

The Bible says that to renew our strength we must "hope in the Lord." We will then "run and not grow weary" and "walk and not grow faint." I know I was given energy and strength for the battles I had to fight each day, and I know that strength came from God.

God did that for me, and he'll do it for you too, but first you must trust Him and hope in Him.

1. How does this relate to your life?

2. What were your little victories this week?

"The most radical act anyone can commit is to be happy."
- Patch Adams

The Importance of Laughter

LAUGHTER IS ESSENTIAL
FOR HEALING

That Patch Adams was really on to something. He knew that laughter was good for the body and the soul and the medical sciences back up that claim.

"Remember laughing?" Adams writes. "Laughter enhances the blood flow to the body's extremities and improves cardiovascular function. Laughter releases endorphins and other natural mood elevating and pain-killing chemicals, improves the transfer of oxygen and nutrients to internal organs . . . Laughter boosts the immune system and helps the body fight off disease, cancer cells as well as viral, bacterial and other infections. Being happy is the best cure of all diseases!"

1. How does this relate to your life?

2. What were your little victories this week?

"I pray also that the eyes of your heart may be enlightened
in order that you may know the hope to which he has called you,
the riches of his glorious inheritance in the saints,
and his incomparably great power for us who believe."
- Ephesians 1:18-20

Soul Food

PRAYING FOR OUR
FRIENDS AND FAMILY

Prayer sustained me during my recovery. There were many complex surgeries I went through and each time prayers went up for me from the world over. I am a living testament to the power of prayer.

The fact is that prayer makes a difference in other people's lives: it grants hope and strength to those we pray for. Remember that we're all on this crazy ride together. Keep up with what's going on in the lives of your friends and family. Make it a point to pray for them when they need help—it accomplishes more than you know.

1. How does this relate to your life?

. . . .

. . . .

. . . .

. . . .

. . . .

. . . .

. . . .

2. What were your little victories this week?

. . . .

. . . .

. . . .

. . . .

. . . .

. . . .

. . . .

"We cannot do great things on this earth, only small things with great love."
– Mother Theresa

Life Without Regrets

---❖---

A FOREVER GIFT

A few years back I hired a neighborhood kid named Alex to mow our lawn. We did this for a few summers until he got to an age where he wanted to move on to bigger and better things. I didn't see him for a while.

The night before my big benefit I was at home waiting to go, sitting impatiently in my wheelchair. There was a knock on the door and I told whoever it was to come in.

Alex stepped in. He'd grown and matured some, but I'd recognize him anywhere. "I'm sorry I can't come tonight," he said. "I just wanted to give you this."

With that he handed me an envelope. I smiled and thanked him, then waited until he was gone to open it. Inside was seven dollars.

The monetary value of the gift? Seven dollars: enough to see a matinee or get a car wash. The value of the gift to me? Incalculable.

1. How does this relate to your life?

. . . .

. . . .

. . . .

. . . .

. . . .

. . . .

2. What were your little victories this week?

. . . .

. . . .

. . . .

. . . .

. . . .

. . . .

. . . .

"Triumphs without difficulties are empty. Indeed; it is difficulties that make the triumph. It is no feat to travel the smooth road."
– Unknown

Endurance

--- ⚙ ---

THERE IS NO TRIUMPH
WITHOUT DIFFICULTY

When you see weightlifters in the gym, what are they doing? Their goal is to get stronger, and to do that they need resistance. They need pushback, and the more the better.

Most people want to be "strong" but also want life to be as easy and trouble-free as possible. In reality those things are mutually exclusive: we become stronger through difficulties and trials. We learn to challenge ourselves and to be real with those around us.

We must have difficulty before we can have triumph.

1. How does this relate to your life?

....

....

....

....

....

....

....

2. What were your little victories this week?

....

....

....

....

....

....

....

....

Finish Strong

NEVER GIVE UP

An interesting quote coming from the man whose last name we use as a synonym for brilliance. Einstein did have a certain degree of genetic gifting, but perhaps not more than others in his grad school: certainly not more than any other physicist in the 20th century.

No, his gift was that of focus and determination. He sought to understand the nature of time and space and he kept going until he reached beyond the stock answers Newton had come up with 400 years earlier.

What is possible if we run hard all the way, not just until we reach a place of comfort and security? We'll never know unless we try.

1. How does this relate to your life?

. . . .

. . . .

. . . .

. . . .

. . . .

. . . .

. . . .

2. What were your little victories this week?

. . . .

. . . .

. . . .

. . . .

. . . .

. . . .

. . . .

"Whether you think that you can or that you can't, you're usually right."
- Henry Ford

Power of a Positive Outlook

SELF-FULFILLING PROPHECY

One of the hallmarks of a positive outlook is that it sees possibility and opportunity where a pessimist might see hardship and closed doors. A positive outlook makes the world larger, expanding possibilities.

If you think you can, you may ask questions that will lead you to places you want to go. If you think you can't, you'll never open up the line of inquiry (why bother, as it is futile?) and you'll never find out what good thing was waiting for you, there for the asking.

Thinking you can leads to trying, and no one ever got anywhere without trying.

1. How does this relate to your life?

. . . .

. . . .

. . . .

. . . .

. . . .

. . . .

. . . .

2. What were your little victories this week?

. . . .

. . . .

. . . .

. . . .

. . . .

. . . .

. . . .

"Todd remembers details about the accident that one would never think he could. As he talked his delivery was so calming. He firmly believes that this experience has a purpose, one far greater than most people could comprehend at this time." – Erica Fultz

Finding Meaning in Suffering

———————— ⚙ ————————

EVERY EXPERIENCE HAS A PURPOSE

Romans 8:28 says, "And we know that in all things God works for the good of those who love him." This doesn't mean God causes bad things to happen to us. What it does mean is that, when bad things happen, God can use them to bring good into our lives.

There's a catch though. Not a big one, really—we just have to be open to the positive. Rather than simply seeing disaster, we have to be on the lookout for ways that God might use this. Will he use it to inspire people and draw people closer together? That's what happened in my case.

My life was enriched immeasurably because of this accident. I was privileged to see the full extent of the love people have for me in a way I never would have been able to otherwise.

1. How does this relate to your life?

....
....
....
....
....
....
....

2. What were your little victories this week?

....
....
....
....
....
....
....
....

"Ever since I can remember I have been afraid of needles and shots. When I heard I'd be getting one, I'd go lightheaded."

One Step at a Time

---✹---

LIVING WITH PURPOSE

A strong sense of priorities has the ability to erase lifelong fears. How incredible is that? Under the right circumstances, your mind doesn't think, it doesn't process—it just *reacts* to what's right, to what you want.

I learned to give myself shots because I had to if I was going to go home. So I did it because I wanted to be with my kids, I wanted to be in my house, and I wanted to be with my wife.

If you want something bad enough, you'll find you can overcome your fears too.

1. How does this relate to your life?

....

....

....

....

....

....

....

2. What were your little victories this week?

....

....

....

....

....

....

....

....

Gratitude

PERSPECTIVE FOR THE AVERAGE DAY

Oftentimes it takes difficult circumstances to draw out the greatness in us: a soldier on the battlefield discovers the measure of his courage, and a pitcher in the World Series discovers how much grit he has and how much sink he can put on his sinker.

But what about the Wednesday when you go to work, come home and make dinner, take the kids to soccer, watch a little TV, and go to bed? What about those days?

Think about this: there are no guarantees in life. You may have occasion to be tested, but while life is going well enjoy it! Enjoy your family and friends, and know that this too shall change. Hopefully you'll be equipped to handle the hard times when they come, and have the perspective to enjoy the good times while they're here.

1. How does this relate to your life?

. . . .

. . . .

. . . .

. . . .

. . . .

. . . .

. . . .

2. What were your little victories this week?

. . . .

. . . .

. . . .

. . . .

. . . .

. . . .

. . . .

"You need to be aware of what others are doing, applaud their efforts, acknowledge their successes, and encourage them in their pursuits. When we all help one another, everybody wins."
– Jim Stovall

Family and Friends

THE POWER OF ENCOURAGEMENT

In my CaringBridge posts, I often said I couldn't have done it without the group that was loving and encouraging me. I may not always have used those precise words, but the intention was certainly there.

That wasn't just a nice thing to say. The encouragement, the prayers and support of our community, was every bit as necessary to my recovery as was the medical care I received.

Think about that. Thoreau said that most men lead lives of quiet desperation. Who around you is in desperate need of encouragement today?

1. How does this relate to your life?

. . . .

. . . .

. . . .

. . . .

. . . .

. . . .

. . . .

2. What were your little victories this week?

. . . .

. . . .

. . . .

. . . .

. . . .

. . . .

. . . .

> *"All that Adam had, all that Caesar could, you have and can do . . . Build, therefore, your own world."*
> *- Ralph Waldo Emerson*

Gold Medals

---　✸　---

OUR MOMENT IS EVERY DAY

In another entry I talked about the magic of the Olympics. Olympians spend four years in training for a few hours of competition, and that is part of the glory of the event. To think of such sacrifice and dedication, well, that's compelling stuff.

Our lives are an event. They are a competition (a lot of times we're competing with ourselves) to do the best we are capable of every day. That goes for work, for play, for our relationships and for our spiritual lives.

If Olympians take a week off to sit on the couch and eat junk food, they won't be able to perform to their capability. The same is true of us. We have within us the potential for greatness, every day. Live up to it.

YEAR OF LITTLE VICTORIES

1. How does this relate to your life?

2. What were your little victories this week?

"Aerodynamically the bumblebee shouldn't be able to fly,
but the bumblebee doesn't know that so it goes on flying anyway."
- Mary Kay Ash

The Miracle of Life

I'M LUCKY TO BE ALIVE
(AND SO ARE YOU)

During the first twenty-four hours after my accident Erica over-heard a couple of people say that folks with injuries like mine aren't supposed to make it. Usually the internal trauma is just too much. Thus, I can say that I'm lucky to be alive.

But we're all lucky to be alive. We're lucky that our parents met at that dance and that their glance across the dance floor turned into a conversation and lead eventually to wedding bells. Life itself is incredibly unlikely to exist. Each and every life, your life and mine, are gifts from God and we should treat them accordingly.

Many of us don't stop and reflect on the big questions, the biggest of which is why am I here at all? Like the bumblebee, we fly because we don't know any better. Stop for a moment and give credit where credit is due. Life is truly a miracle, so we should treat it with rever-ence and respect, both for our lives and others.

1. How does this relate to your life?

....

....

....

....

....

....

....

2. What were your little victories this week?

....

....

....

....

....

....

....

....

"God whispers to us in our pleasures, speaks to us in our conscience, but shouts in our pains: It is His megaphone to rouse a deaf world."
– C.S. Lewis

The Spiritual Life

--- ⚙ ---

GOD IS WITH US IN OUR PAIN

Many of us in this country are spiritually hard of hearing. Sometimes it takes a calamity to get us to slow down and engage in some introspection. And there's certainly nothing like a calamity to realign your priorities.

God walks with us in this process. He certainly held me up during my recovery. I felt God's presence, and I know that he blessed me and my family. I felt his presence in the love my family and friends showed me. It was truly an incredible experience, and I certainly wouldn't have had it, if not for the accident.

1. How does this relate to your life?

. . . .

. . . .

. . . .

. . . .

. . . .

. . . .

. . . .

2. What were your little victories this week?

. . . .

. . . .

. . . .

. . . .

. . . .

. . . .

. . . .

The Importance of Laughter

WHEN HISTORY IS A FUNNY THING

Take half an hour or so and sit down with a cup of coffee (or tea, if that's your cup). Funny stories from our past have a way of bonding the teller and the listener with each successive recounting.

Write down some of the funny stories you can remember from your childhood. If it helps, get together with a sibling or childhood friend so you can play off each other. Most of us had a great many funny occurrences in our growing up years that we've all but forgotten about in our hectic lives.

Write these stories down. Get together with your kids, turn off the TV, and tell them the stories.

1. How does this relate to your life?

....

....

....

....

....

....

....

2. What were your little victories this week?

....

....

....

....

....

....

....

....

"But I tell you: Love your enemies and pray for those who persecute you, that you may be sons of your Father in heaven. He causes his sun to rise on the evil and the good, and sends rain on the righteous and the unrighteous."
– Matthew 5:44-45

Soul Food

--- ❖ ---

PRAYING FOR YOUR ENEMIES

Enemies were more common back in the days when people routinely went after each other with swords. These days that's considerably less common, though we do often have people who do us wrong in other ways.

Jesus tells us to love them and pray for them, because we are to imitate God. If God had not loved us while we were his enemies, we could never have become his children. We are to extend the same courtesy to others as God extended to us.

Anyone can find God, and that divine spark is in all of us. Treat each other accordingly.

1. How does this relate to your life?

. . . .

. . . .

. . . .

. . . .

. . . .

. . . .

. . . .

2. What were your little victories this week?

. . . .

. . . .

. . . .

. . . .

. . . .

. . . .

. . . .

. . . .

"Todd has talked many times to me—and I am sure most of you—about life without regrets, and I am seeing it at work right now. It is such a blessing to have each of you write in."
—Erica Fultz

Life Without Regrets

❋

FRIENDS

I think often about regrets and trying not to have them. One thing I'm sure I would regret is letting my friends and family down. Of course, I'm not perfect and I have let people down in the past, and so I know the pain that can cause for both parties.

I've resolved to do what I can to support my friends and family in whatever way I can. I've committed to this and I've always tried to do it to the best of my ability.

How do you measure success in this endeavor? At the end of the day, if I have a good relationship with them and I'm 110% that they know I care for them, I consider that a success.

1. How does this relate to your life?

....

....

....

....

....

....

....

2. What were your little victories this week?

....

....

....

....

....

....

....

....

"I knew I was traveling down a long road. I found something positive each day, focusing on that thing to get by."

Endurance

A POSITIVE EACH DAY

Every day we are presented with a choice: do we dwell on the negatives or focus on the positives?

Life is always a mixed bag. I very rarely have a day that is all bad or all good. You get a little of both, and you can choose how you process that information. Consider the negatives: let's say you focused on those day in and day out, year in and year out, for your whole life. What kind of a life would that be? It would be gloomy, friendless, joyless, and full of defeat.

Now let's say you focus on the positives: every day brings you good news. Sure, some days are harder than others, but there's always something good you can latch onto. A life like that will be marked by joy, friendship, inspiration, and success.

1. How does this relate to your life?

....

....

....

....

....

....

....

2. What were your little victories this week?

....

....

....

....

....

....

....

....

Finish Strong

--- ❖ ---

MARRIAGE

Marriage is a forever thing, a for-better-or-worse thing. Any marriage that lasts longer than a year will see good times and bad times: that's just the human condition. No one is immune, and no relationship is immune.

When hard times come, it is of the utmost importance to stand by your husband or wife. It is then that they need you most. I am so thankful that Erica was so strong through all of this. She was with me every step of the way. I couldn't have done it without her.

1. How does this relate to your life?

....

....

....

....

....

....

....

2. What were your little victories this week?

....

....

....

....

....

....

....

....

"It's strange to feel simultaneously lucky and unlucky. I marveled at this oddity of having both of those emotions colliding within myself. What were the odds that I would live? Why did I survive?"

Power of a Positive Outlook

❈

LUCKY AND UNLUCKY

I've always believed that each experience we go through has a purpose. My accident had some negative ramifications for my life—that much is sure—but it has also enriched me in incredible ways. Why dwell on what I lost? What good can come from that?

I could look at it as an incredibly bad stroke of luck that I was hit head on driving down Manning Avenue: but doing so would be a sure route to misery. Instead I have chosen to see myself as incredibly fortunate. Statistically, I shouldn't have survived that. Now I see every day as an incredible gift, a chance to be with my wife and children. Life is beautiful and grand, and I'm thankful I was spared.

1. How does this relate to your life?

....

....

....

....

....

....

....

2. What were your little victories this week?

....

....

....

....

....

....

....

....

*"Sometimes you just have to embrace the truth
no matter how difficult. Reality can be harsh, but I would rather
meet it head on than hide from it. "*

Finding Meaning in Suffering

EMBRACING DIFFICULT TRUTHS

I remember the feeling I had when I first saw the X-rays of my reconstructed ankle. It looked like a construction project, nothing natural about it. It was disheartening.

This, of course, takes nothing away from the good work the surgeon did: without that work I wouldn't be walking today. After seeing it, I had to accept that as the reality of my situation. Obviously Plan A involves the ankle God gave me, and I was able to stay on Plan A for over forty years.

But sometimes Plan B comes along. You can drown your sorrows, or you can grieve the loss, accept it, and move on with your life.

1. How does this relate to your life?

....

....

....

....

....

....

....

2. What were your little victories this week?

....

....

....

....

....

....

....

....

"All right, that's over, I thought. Now let's go live."

One Step at a Time

✦

CLOSURE

The walking party was great. We held it on June 5, 2009, a year to the day after I was hit. It's important to have a big event at the end of a significant era. The event signals a turning point. It is simultaneously and end and a beginning.

Looking back on it, I'm glad we went that way with it. If we had done nothing, I might have lingered in that state—the "accident victim" state—indefinitely. I wanted to no longer be Todd, the accident victim. I wanted to just be Todd.

1. How does this relate to your life?

2. What were your little victories this week?

"It is a very powerful and humbling thing, meeting with someone who helped to save your life and put your body back together."

Gratitude

❁

RELYING ON OTHERS

Many Americans today are caught up in the notion of the rugged individualist. We believe we're self-sufficient and don't need anybody. In some circles the notion of needing others is seen as weakness.

After my accident, I was reduced to complete helplessness. I needed quick and capable intervention to save my life, then a number of very long surgeries to restore my body to some semblance of wholeness. I needed others to come out and take care of the things I would normally do. I had to rely on people.

And you know what? It was fabulous. I learned that not only will other people help, they'll be glad to do it. When you really need help, it's OK to ask for it.

1. How does this relate to your life?

....

....

....

....

....

....

....

2. What were your little victories this week?

....

....

....

....

....

....

....

....

"Sitting in my own room alone, I had a lot of time for reflection. My thoughts often drifted to my younger brother, Tim. I thought of how many challenges he faced and overcame when he was alive. I remembered how much he taught me."

Family and Friends

REMEMBERING THE EXAMPLE OF THOSE WHO'VE GONE BEFORE

We've all had people who have gone before us, people we can remember and whose example we can look to for guidance. For me, I remembered my brother, Tim. He endured his cancer with dignity, he loved greatly and he never gave up.

Those qualities were vital for me as I recovered. No matter how bad things got, I knew I could do it. I knew because I'd seen Tim endure and keep fighting twenty-five years before. In the way he fought and the way he loved he gave me a gift of immeasurable worth.

1. How does this relate to your life?

....

....

....

....

....

....

....

2. What were your little victories this week?

....

....

....

....

....

....

....

....

"I was taken by the beauty of the closing of the Olympics too. It's amazing how long and hard the athletes work with their eyes on the goal. I'm sure there are days when they just feel like giving up, not getting up early, not working out, not eating right, but they have to keep persevering in order to win."
– Livija Ford

Gold Medals

--- ❖ ---

EYES ON THE PRIZE

Livija Ford wrote that in the Guestbook on my CaringBridge site. She was responding to an entry in which I had been overcome with emotion as I watched the closing ceremonies of the Beijing Olympics.

I wrote, "As I thought about it, I realized that we have all trained very hard and long for our moment too, but our moment happens every day. It is being a great parent, spouse, and friend. It is helping those around us and being a good role model. It is our passions and experiences, our faith, and our legacy."

An Olympian's moment is a fleeting one, but ours happens all the time each day. Our gold medals are the people we invest in. Some of them are bright and shiny, some need a little dusting off, but we have them and wear them around our necks every day.

1. How does this relate to your life?

....

....

....

....

....

....

....

2. What were your little victories this week?

....

....

....

....

....

....

....

....

"It's crucial to take the time to notice these simple things. Slow down. Live those moments of stillness. I drive down the road at the end of a long day and I see a stunning sunset. I watch while the other cars drive hurriedly onward, and I think how we ought to, all of us, be pulling over onto the side of the road taking this in."

The Miracle of Life

---❖---

THE SIMPLE THINGS

There's something to be said for recovery. It takes life from its typically breakneck speed down to a speed usually reserved for monks. While this has certain drawbacks, there are certain benefits as well: the biggest one is noticing and appreciating things I never really paid attention to before.

Now clearly, I'm not saying that you all quit your jobs and check into a monastery. What I am saying is take ten minutes to sit outside with a cup of coffee or tea and just be. Just listen and watch and reflect.

Allow some openness in your life for God to speak to you.

1. How does this relate to your life?

....

....

....

....

....

....

....

2. What were your little victories this week?

....

....

....

....

....

....

....

....

The Spritual Life

--- ✿ ---

APPEARANCES

On December 7, 2008, I developed a surgical hernia. Things dropped and shifted, and all of a sudden I had this crazy unsightly bulge in my stomach. I had been disfigured.

While coming to terms with that, I wrote this: "You know, we all have things about us that may not look right or that we are unhappy with. There are many people who judge us for what we have or don't have or how we look, or walk, or talk. God judges us only by who we are and how we treat people, how we help those less fortunate. Do we cast stones or do we heal the sick? Do we take advantage of the weak, or do we share a few fishes and loaves of bread so hundreds can eat?"

God, as it turns out, is far less concerned with appearances than we are. He cares about what's in your heart.

1. How does this relate to your life?

. . . .

. . . .

. . . .

. . . .

. . . .

. . . .

. . . .

2. What were your little victories this week?

. . . .

. . . .

. . . .

. . . .

. . . .

. . . .

. . . .

. . . .

*"It's okay to laugh. It's okay to be silly.
Often it's absolutely necessary."*

The Importance of Laughter

THE PSYCHOLOGICAL BENEFITS
OF THE BELLY LAUGH

In *The Year of Little Victories* I wrote, "We only get a certain amount of time on this earth, so we may as well have a little fun, no matter what the hardship is that you're dealing with. It's something each of us can afford."

According to the American Association for Theraputic Humor, many people are in the bad habit of stockpiling negative emotions like anger, sadness, and fear. When held inside these negative emotions cause biochemical reactions that adversely affect our bodies. Laughter allows us to release those emotions: it provides catharsis. The psychological benefits of regular, long, sustained laughter are quite substantial. Plus it's fun!

When life becomes hard, you literally *need* to laugh.

1. How does this relate to your life?

. . . .

. . . .

. . . .

. . . .

. . . .

. . . .

. . . .

2. What were your little victories this week?

. . . .

. . . .

. . . .

. . . .

. . . .

. . . .

. . . .

"Just know that many people are praying for your recovery and rejoicing in the miracle that you are still counted among the living. We thank God for that blessing."

Soul Food

***

THANK GOD!

God doesn't owe us anything and life isn't fair. Anything we get from God is something he gave us out of goodness, not because we deserved it.

It makes sense then that we should be thankful to Him, just as we would offer our thanks to a generous uncle who handed down a family heirloom. Most of you reading this book are very, very blessed when you look at it in a global perspective. We have a lot to be thankful for, and the act of thankfulness tunes our hearts toward God.

1. How does this relate to your life?

. . . .

. . . .

. . . .

. . . .

. . . .

. . . .

. . . .

2. What were your little victories this week?

. . . .

. . . .

. . . .

. . . .

. . . .

. . . .

. . . .

"It is so rewarding to be around family. It is amazing how much you grow together when you have the time to be together. It is time you never regret."

Life Without Regrets

--- ⚙ ---

MAKING TIME FOR FAMILY

Shortly after the above quote, I wrote, "I hope you are finding the time in this busy life to be around those you love. I've been blessed with another three months off work to spend at home. I will look back at these recovery days with fond memories: a little bit of pain but a lot of love."

How many people—how many guys—will ever get an opportunity to spend three uninterrupted months with their kids while they are little? I daresay very few. These are times I treasure. There's just no substitute for time with your kids. There's no such thing as bonding on the fast track. We may be used to doing things on a business schedule, but kid's lives are ruled by playing and eating and sleeping. They have time for things, and if we're going to connect with them, we had better have time for things too.

1. How does this relate to your life?

. . . .

. . . .

. . . .

. . . .

. . . .

. . . .

. . . .

2. What were your little victories this week?

. . . .

. . . .

. . . .

. . . .

. . . .

. . . .

. . . .

*"Each of us has the capacity to think we've got it worst of all.
We can put blinders on and get caught up in our own struggles."*

Endurance

--- ✿ ---

PUT YOUR TROUBLES
IN PERSPECTIVE

When I started going to the Courage Center, I started meeting others who were struggling just as much, if not more, than I was. I felt amazed at their strength and humbled in their midst.

There are many people around the world struggling to feed their families and to provide basic shelter. Most of us in America are insulated from these concerns. We may have troubles (and they may be real troubles), but it is comforting to know that, for those of us in the middle of it, you are not the only one. After my accident other accident victims in various stages of recovery reached out to me on CaringBridge to share their experiences. We're a big, connected web of humanity. If you're struggling, know that you're not struggling alone. Reach out.

1. How does this relate to your life?

. . . .

. . . .

. . . .

. . . .

. . . .

. . . .

. . . .

2. What were your little victories this week?

. . . .

. . . .

. . . .

. . . .

. . . .

. . . .

. . . .

"We can't all leave a prestigious background or lots of money to our children, but we can leave them a legacy of love."
– Naomi Rhode

Finish Strong

❀

WHAT THEY'LL SAY
WHEN I'M GONE

Life comes to a predictable conclusion: we pass. An accident like the one I went through convinces you of your own mortality. What matters in the end isn't how much money or property or prestige we leave our kids: it's how much love we leave them. The examples we set for them in our relationships will serve them well or will haunt them during their adult lives.

Our present day actions echo into eternity. Leave them a legacy of love, of hope, of positive thinking, of security in who they are. If you've done that, you've done your job.

1. How does this relate to your life?

. . . .

. . . .

. . . .

. . . .

. . . .

. . . .

. . . .

2. What were your little victories this week?

. . . .

. . . .

. . . .

. . . .

. . . .

. . . .

. . . .

Your YEAR OF LITTLE VICTORIES

Pick your biggest victory of the week and write them out here.
This is your trophy case for the year!

1 ....

2 ....

3 ....

4 ....

5 ....

6 ....

7 ....

8 ....

9 ....

10 ....

11 ....

12 ....

13 ....

14 ....

15 ....

16 ....

17 ....

18 ....

19 ....

20 ....

21 ....

22 ....

23 ....

24 ....

25 ....

26 ....

27 ....

28 ....

29 ....

30 ....

31 ....

32 ....

33 ....

34 ....

35 . . . .

36 . . . .

37 . . . .

38 . . . .

39 . . . .

40 . . . .

41 . . . .

42 . . . .

43 . . . .

44 . . . .

45 . . . .

46 . . . .

47 . . . .

48 . . . .

49 . . . .

50 . . . .

50 . . . .

51 . . . .

52 . . . .